I0817034

CAREERS CUT SHORT

BY BRIAN HALL

THE WILD WORLD OF SPORTS

SportsZone
An Imprint of Abdo Publishing
abdopublishing.com

abdopublishing.com

Published by Abdo Publishing, a division of ABDO, PO Box 398166, Minneapolis, Minnesota 55439.

Printed in the United States of America, North Mankato, Minnesota
102017
012018

Cover Photos: Gary Stewart/AP Images, foreground; Roy Dabner/AP Images, background
Interior Photos: AP Images, 4, 21, 22, 29, 31, 32, 35; Bettmann/Getty Images, 6, 45; Murray Becker/AP Images, 7; Al Golub/AP Images, 9; Leonard Ignelzi/AP Images, 10; Al Messerschmidt/AP Images, 11, 36; Eric Risberg/AP Images, 13; Kevin Terrell/AP Images, 14; Roy Dabner/AP Images, 16; Matt York/AP Images, 17; Nathan Bilow/AP Images, 19; David Smith/AP Images, 23; Clark/AP Images, 25; Vernon Biever/AP Images, 26; B. Bennett/Bruce Bennett/Getty Images, 38; Rusty Kennedy/AP Images, 39; Tony Tomsic/AP Images, 41; R. J. Carson/AP Images, 43

Editor: Patrick Donnelly
Series Designer: Craig Hinton

Publisher's Cataloging-in-Publication Data

Names: Hall, Brian, author.
Title: Careers cut short / by Brian Hall.
Description: Minneapolis, Minnesota : Abdo Publishing, 2018. | Series: The wild world of sports | Includes online resources and index.
Identifiers: LCCN 2017946934 | ISBN 9781532113635 (lib.bdg.) | ISBN 9781532152511 (ebook)
Subjects: LCSH: Sports--United States--History--Juvenile literature. | Sports--Miscellanea--Juvenile literature.
Classification: DDC 796--dc23
LC record available at https://lccn.loc.gov/2017946934

TABLE OF CONTENTS

THE IRON HORSE

The history of sports is marked by many athletes who died or suffered devastating injuries or illnesses that shortened their careers. One of the most famous was New York Yankees Hall of Fame first baseman Lou Gehrig.

Gehrig stood in front of a microphone at Yankee Stadium on July 4, 1939, and declared himself "the luckiest man on the face of the earth." Those were surprising words from somebody forced to retire because of a disease called amyotrophic lateral sclerosis (ALS).

Gehrig was a shining example of strength in baseball, for both his 493 career home runs and his streak of playing in 2,130 straight games. The man who was known as the "Iron Horse" for his durability won the Triple Crown in 1934 by leading the American League (AL) with 49 home runs, 166 runs batted in, and a .363 batting average. He also helped the Yankees become baseball's first dynasty, winning six World Series between 1927 and 1938.

The classic left-handed swing of Lou Gehrig produced 493 career home runs.

Gehrig watches from the Yankees dugout on May 2, 1939, as he sits out for the first time in 14 years.

But Gehrig knew something was wrong in 1939. He felt weak and uncoordinated during spring training. When the season began, he had just four hits—all singles—in 28 at-bats through the first eight games.

Gehrig took himself out of the lineup on May 2, 1939. He wouldn't play another game. Six weeks later, doctors at the Mayo Clinic in Rochester, Minnesota, diagnosed his illness. ALS affects the nerve cells in the brain and spinal cord and leads to the inability to control muscle movement.

MISSING MUNSON

The Yankees have seen their share of tragedy. After Lou Gehrig died, the team waited 37 years to name another captain. But, like Gehrig before him, catcher Thurman Munson's career ended in tragedy. He was the 1970 AL Rookie of the Year and 1976 AL Most Valuable Player (MVP). But Munson was killed in a plane crash on August 2, 1979. He was just 32 years old.

Gehrig immediately announced his retirement. He was 37 years old. Just a year earlier he had still been one of the best players in baseball. His rapid decline shocked fans and fellow players. The Yankees held "Lou Gehrig Day" on July 4 to honor him and allow him to thank his fans. He died less than two years later.

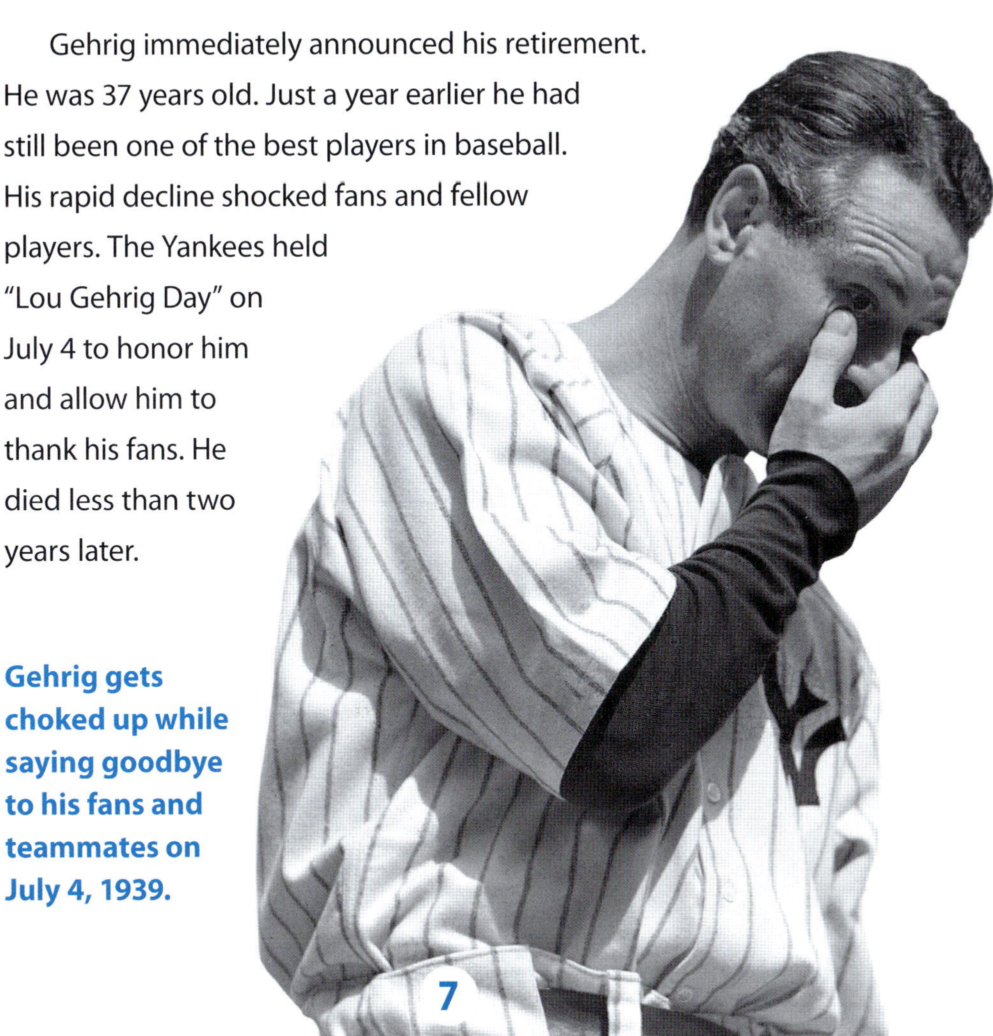

Gehrig gets choked up while saying goodbye to his fans and teammates on July 4, 1939.

BO KNOWS

Few athletes captured America's attention like Bo Jackson. Born Vincent Edward Jackson, the multisport star became one of the most marketed athletes of his time. Nike's "Bo Knows" advertising campaign made Jackson a household name in the late 1980s.

Jackson lived up to the hype on the field. At Auburn University he was a sprinter on the track-and-field team and a dominating baseball player. But he really stood out as a running back on the Tigers football team. Jackson won the Heisman Trophy, given to the best player in college football. He was the first pick in the 1986 National Football League (NFL) draft, selected by the Tampa Bay Buccaneers. But Jackson never signed with the Buccaneers. He chose to play baseball instead.

The New York Yankees had drafted Jackson out of high school, but he decided to go to Auburn instead. In a later draft the Kansas City Royals picked Jackson, and this time he joined them.

Bo Jackson tore through NFL defenses with the Los Angeles Raiders.

He displayed a blend of speed and power that had rarely been seen in the sport. Jackson was an All-Star and a top-10 in MVP voting in 1989 after hitting 32 home runs and stealing 26 bases.

And in the days before "going viral," sports highlight shows were filled with Jackson's amazing plays. He once threw out a runner at home plate while standing on the warning track 300 feet (91 m) away. He thrilled fans when he blasted a 450-foot (137-m) home run on the first pitch he saw in the 1989 All-Star Game.

But Jackson had not entirely given up on football. He signed with the Los Angeles Raiders and made his NFL debut in 1987. Jackson played a limited football schedule, joining the Raiders once baseball season finished in early October. His speed and power made him unique on the football field, too. Jackson rushed for 950 yards in just 11 games in 1989.

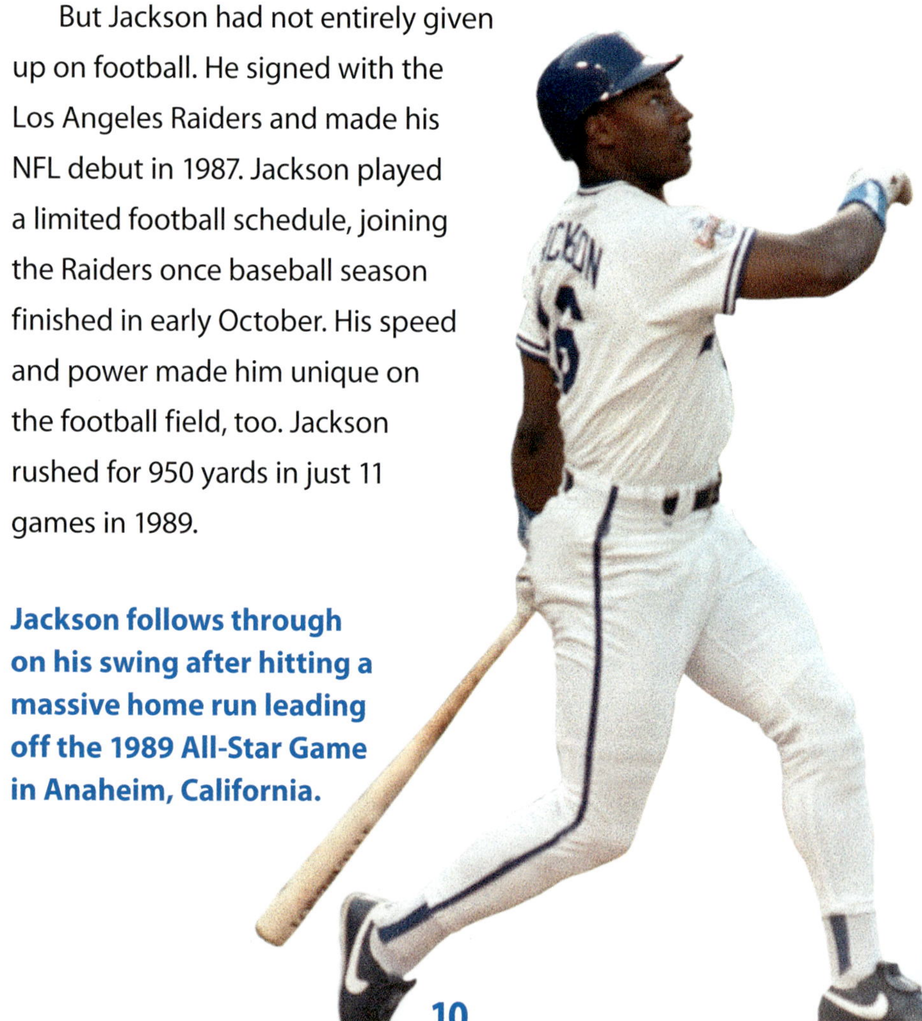

Jackson follows through on his swing after hitting a massive home run leading off the 1989 All-Star Game in Anaheim, California.

Jackson injured his hip on this play, which turned out to be his last in the NFL.

Jackson's career will always be discussed in terms of what might have been. He suffered a dislocated hip while being tackled in a playoff game in January 1991. He never played football again. He returned to the baseball diamond, but he wasn't the same player. He'd lost too much of his speed to be effective. Jackson's career was over after four years in football and eight years in baseball. But the memories he created in that short span will be the stuff of legend.

KNICKERS AND TAM

Payne Stewart had a flair for the dramatic, from seizing big moments on the golf course to his stylish attire. Stewart was known for dressing in knee-high knickerbocker pants and a cap called a tam o' shanter. He had won three major championships by the age of 42. His fist pump after sinking a putt to win the 1999 US Open at Pinehurst is one of golf's most memorable images.

However, Stewart died in a strange airplane accident a few weeks after helping the US team win the Ryder Cup in 1999. He and five others were traveling from Florida to Texas. The plane lost contact with air traffic control and didn't make an anticipated turn.

Fighter jets were dispatched to check on Stewart's plane. Its windows had frosted over, indicating a problem with the plane's oxygen system. Everyone on board was likely already dead. The plane ran out of fuel and crashed in a South Dakota field. Stewart was 42 years old.

Stewart was a fashionable and enthusiastic figure on the pro golf tour.

Riddell
40

ATHLETE TURNED SOLDIER

Many athletes have no say in how their careers end. Not Pat Tillman. He chose to give up his spot in the NFL as he was entering the prime of his career. The former Arizona State University standout played four seasons as a safety for the Arizona Cardinals. He started the final 28 games of his career. Tillman was known as the hard-hitting, vocal leader in the Cardinals' defensive backfield.

Tillman will forever be known as more than a football player. He said he was so personally affected by the September 11, 2001, terrorist attacks on the United States that he had to do something. At age 25, Tillman decided he couldn't play football while his country was fighting a war.

Tillman was a star safety for the Arizona Cardinals.

Tillman passed up a chance to sign a three-year, $3.6 million contract with the Cardinals to enlist in the Army with his brother, Kevin. Kevin Tillman gave up his own athletic career. He played minor league baseball in the Cleveland Indians organization.

In 2002 Pat Tillman became an Army Ranger and was deployed to Iraq. Eventually Tillman, his brother, and fellow Rangers were sent to Afghanistan. In April 2004 their squad came under fire, and Pat Tillman was killed. The Army originally announced that he had died after a firefight with enemy soldiers. It was later revealed he was shot by friendly fire when fellow rangers mistook him for an enemy along a ridge. Tillman was awarded the Purple Heart and Silver Star after his death.

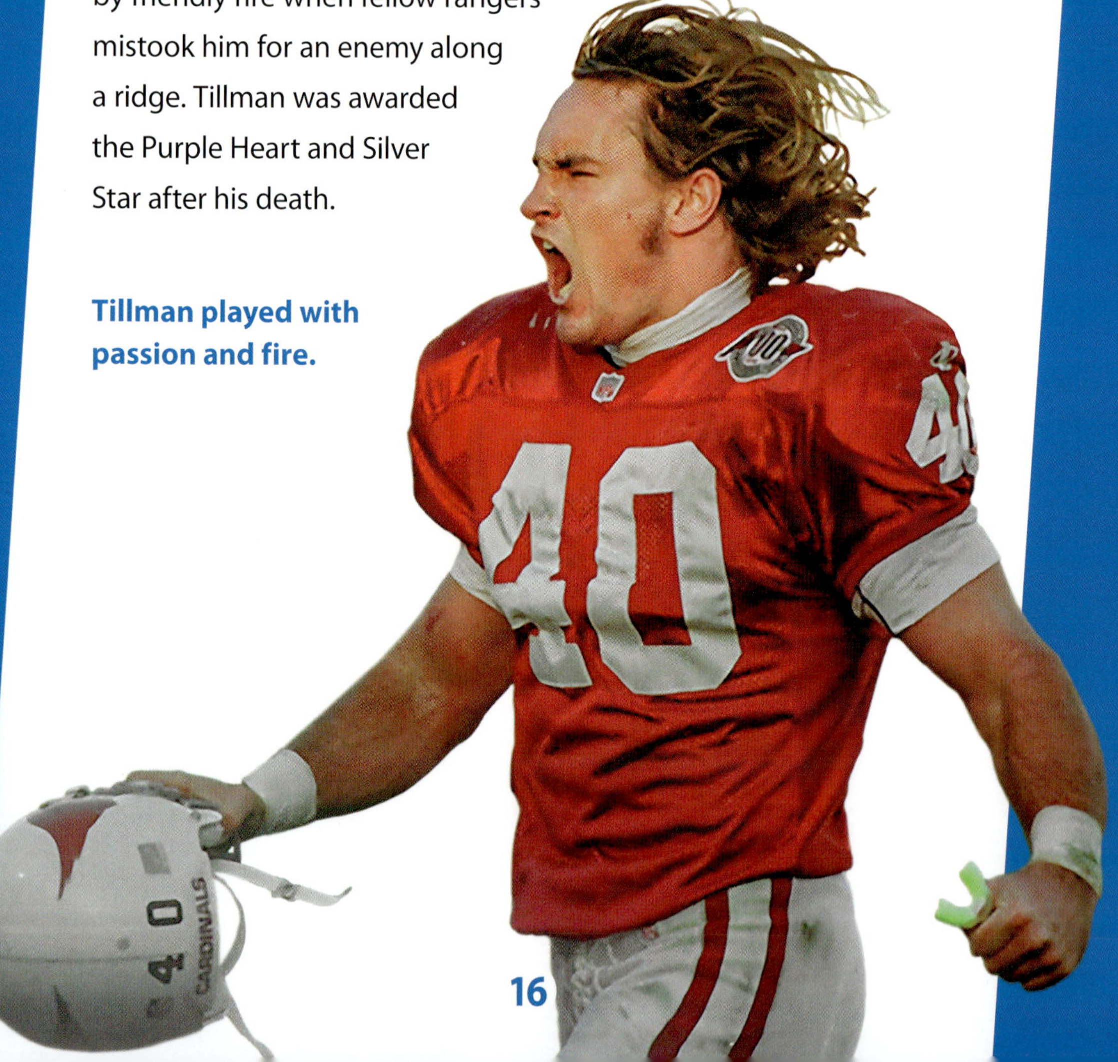

Tillman played with passion and fire.

The Cardinals retired Tillman's jersey in 2004.

PROUD TO SERVE

Wars have shortened the careers of many athletes, even those who were able to return to the field. Ted Williams is seen as one of the greatest hitters ever. The former Boston Red Sox star won two AL MVP awards. But he fell short of 3,000 career hits. Williams might have reached that mark had he not missed the 1943–45 seasons while fighting in World War II and most of the 1952 and 1953 seasons while in the Korean War. Cleveland Indians pitcher Bob Feller enlisted in the US Navy after the bombing of Pearl Harbor in 1941. He missed all or part of four seasons. Feller won 266 games and was in the top 10 in MVP voting six times.

X GAMES PIONEER

Sarah Burke was a pioneer among women in extreme sports. Burke was a Canadian freestyle skier who excelled in the superpipe. She was a six-time champion at the Winter X Games, and in 2007 she was named the female action sports athlete of the year at the ESPY Awards.

Burke pushed for the X Games to add women's freestyle skiing and later successfully lobbied for the halfpipe to be added to the Winter Olympics skiing competition. The event gained acceptance and debuted at the Sochi Olympics in 2014. Burke would have been the gold-medal favorite, but she never got the chance to compete.

Burke crashed near the end of a training run on the halfpipe in Utah in 2012. She landed on her head, and the impact caused bleeding in her brain. She died nine days later at the age of 29.

Sarah Burke flies high during the 2009 Winter X Games.

Jeep
ESPN
WINTER

CHAPTER 6

THE LEFT ARM OF GOD

Sandy Koufax was widely considered the best left-handed pitcher of his generation. Some believe Koufax was the best pitcher ever, period. He was often referred to as "The Left Arm of God."

Koufax began his career with the Brooklyn Dodgers in 1955 when he was 19 years old. He was a hard-throwing pitching prospect who had problems with his control. In his first two seasons he walked almost as many batters as he struck out. In 1958 the Dodgers relocated to Los Angeles, and that's where Koufax hit his stride. He led the National League (NL) in strikeouts in 1961. He had the league's best earned-run average (ERA) the next season. Then he really got rolling.

Between 1963 and 1966 Koufax won the Cy Young Award as the best pitcher in major league baseball three times. He also won

Sandy Koufax delivers a pitch at Philadelphia's Connie Mack Stadium in 1963.

32

PRIOR'S PROBLEMS

Plenty of pitching wonders haven't lived up to the hype. Few came with the publicity and potential of Mark Prior. The second pick in the 2001 Major League Baseball (MLB) draft was a can't-miss pitching prospect. The right-hander was said to have the perfect delivery and wouldn't deal with arm trouble. But upon joining the Chicago Cubs in 2002, Prior racked up high pitch counts and assorted injuries, and his MLB career lasted just five seasons.

the NL MVP Award in 1963. That season he led the league with 25 wins, a 1.88 ERA, 306 strikeouts, and 11 shutouts. Koufax was the NL MVP runner-up two other times and had the lowest ERA in the NL in each of his last five seasons.

He became the first player to pitch four no-hitters and win three Cy Young Awards. Koufax was an All-Star each of his final six seasons.

Koufax holds four baseballs to represent his four career no-hitters after he threw a perfect game against the Chicago Cubs on September 9, 1965.

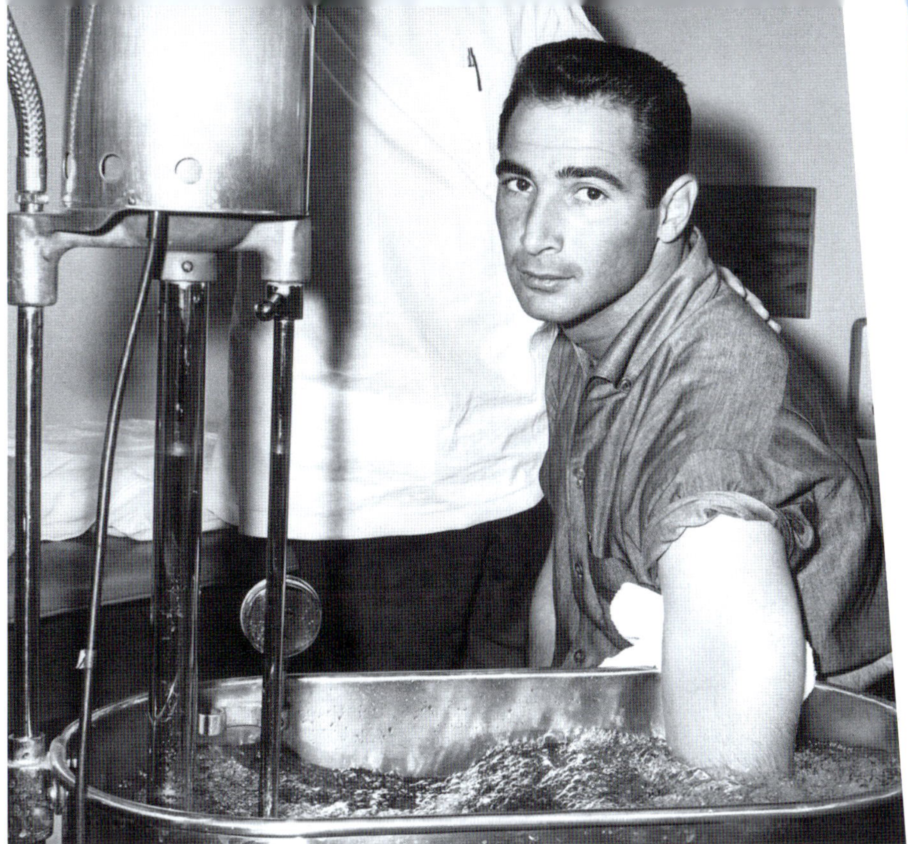

Koufax uses an ice bath to treat his sore left arm. Chronic pain in his pitching arm led to a premature retirement at age 30.

The Dodgers rode him to World Series titles in 1963 and 1965 before losing to the Baltimore Orioles in 1966.

But the left arm that had made him a legend was giving him problems. He was pitching through a lot of pain. Traumatic arthritis in his elbow forced Koufax to retire at the age of 30. He made the decision to walk away from the game after 12 seasons instead of continuing to pitch in pain while risking permanent disability.

His career was cut short, but his legend has not faded. In 1972 Koufax became the youngest player inducted into the Baseball Hall of Fame. He was selected in his first year on the ballot.

LONG-DISTANCE LEGEND

A distance runner from a tiny town in Oregon became one of the most unconventional athletic celebrities in the United States. Steve Prefontaine set a national high school record for the 2-mile race in the late 1960s and became a top college recruit.

Prefontaine decided to stay in his home state and attend the University of Oregon. It proved to be a good fit. The man fans called "Pre" was an aggressive runner. He liked to push the pace instead of sitting back in the pack. And he wasn't afraid to rile up his opponents with trash talk. That approach led him to win seven college national titles for the Ducks. He held 15 American distance running records from 2 miles to 10,000 meters. He even ran in the 1972 Olympics. Prefontaine also fought for the rights of amateur athletes against the Amateur Athletic Union (AAU).

Prefontaine's celebrity also grew through his association with Nike. Oregon track-and-field coach Bill Bowerman was a cofounder of the shoe company, along with Phil Knight. Prefontaine was the first star runner signed by Nike, and he helped publicize the brand.

Steve Prefontaine ran in Adidas during his college days.

However, he didn't live to see Nike become the massive success it is today. Prefontaine died on May 30, 1975, when the car he was driving flipped over in Eugene, Oregon. He was 24 years old.

THE KANSAS COMET

Two great running backs set the standard for the Chicago Bears. Walter Payton became known for his durability during the 1970s and 1980s. He missed just one game over 13 seasons. Playing mostly in the 1960s, fellow Hall of Famer Gale Sayers didn't have the same luck with injuries.

Sayers was speedy, elusive, and an all-around threat. After starring in college at the University of Kansas, he was a first-team All-Pro choice in his first five seasons with the Bears. He was also a league-leading kickoff returner. In 1965 Sayers put his speed and flashy moves on full display. He scored 22 touchdowns and amassed 2,272 total yards to win the NFL Rookie of the Year Award. He scored six touchdowns in one game against the San Francisco 49ers that season.

The next season Sayers rushed for a career-high 1,231 yards. But two years later the injuries began to pile up. A knee injury ended his

Gale Sayers shows off his breakaway speed in a 1967 game.

Sayers is carried off the field after tearing ligaments in his right knee on November 10, 1968.

season with five games to go. Sayers returned to earn Comeback Player of the Year honors in 1969. Another knee injury kept him out of all but four games over the next two seasons, and he retired at age 28, having played only 68 games over seven NFL seasons.

Sayers remains the NFL's all-time leader in kickoff return average at 30.6 yards per attempt. In 1977, at age 34, he became the youngest inductee into the Pro Football Hall of Fame.

Sayers also became known for his strong friendship with fellow Bears running back Brian Piccolo, which was documented in the movie *Brian's Song*. Sayers was black, and Piccolo was white. The two became close friends despite the racial tensions of the time. Piccolo's career was also cut short, after he was diagnosed with cancer. He died in 1970 at age 26.

ANOTHER SHORT RIDE

Terrell Davis is another running back who overcame a short career to make it to the Hall of Fame. Davis was on two Super Bowl–winning teams with the Denver Broncos and was the Super Bowl MVP in January 1998. He was the NFL MVP in 1998 after becoming the fourth player ever to rush for more than 2,000 yards in a season. But he played just 17 more games over the next three seasons before retiring at age 29.

40

CHAPTER 9

BIG RED

His long red hair held back by his familiar headband and a bushy beard made Bill Walton one of the most unique and easily recognizable basketball players in the world. His talent made him one of the best players in college and professional basketball history. But his feet would keep him from fulfilling his potential.

Walton won the James Naismith Award—given to the best college player in the nation—in each of his three seasons at the University of California, Los Angeles (UCLA). The Bruins were undefeated and won the national title in each of his first two years. Walton was masterful with the ball close to the hoop. His array of moves frustrated opponents trying to defend him. And he was a brilliant passer, beating double teams by hitting open teammates for layups.

The Portland Trail Blazers selected Walton with the No. 1 pick in the 1974 National Basketball Association (NBA) draft. Foot injuries hampered him immediately. He played only 35 games as a rookie.

Bill Walton leaps high above the Indiana defense to score a basket in the 1973 national semifinals.

Walton, *right,* blocks the shot of the Denver Nuggets' Dan Issel in 1977.

Yet two years later he led Portland to the NBA title in 1976–77 and was named the NBA Finals MVP. The next season he won the league MVP award, averaging 18.9 points, 13.2 rebounds, 5.0 assists, and 2.5 blocked shots per game.

Walton sat out a season in a dispute with the Trail Blazers regarding what he believed was mistreatment of his injuries by the team's doctors. He lost two full seasons to injury after being traded to the San Diego Clippers. Walton found his way to Boston and helped the Celtics win a championship as the NBA's Sixth Man of the Year in 1985–86. He played in 80 games that season, almost double his previous career average. But more foot issues forced his retirement in 1987. Walton missed nearly 56 percent of his teams' regular-season games in his 13 NBA seasons.

BIG-MAN BLUES

The Blazers have had trouble with highly drafted centers. They selected University of Kentucky center Sam Bowie second overall in 1984. He battled numerous injuries during his five seasons in Portland. That was bad enough. The fact that they chose Bowie over Michael Jordan added insult to injury. Greg Oden was the top pick in the 2007 draft. He played just 82 games in his career for the Blazers because of knee injuries.

LITTLE MO

In a sport that has seen many teen prodigies, tennis star Maureen "Mo" Connolly stands out from the crowd. Few players of any age could match her achievements at the peak of her career. In 1951 Connolly won the US women's national singles championship (now the US Open). She was just 16 years old. It was the first of three straight US singles titles for Connolly and the first of 12 major championships.

Connolly would go on to win the Grand Slam of women's tennis with four major championships in the same season in 1953. And she did it at the age of 18. She was the first woman to accomplish the feat and one of just three women in history through 2017 to have done it.

Connolly's career included nine major singles championships, two doubles titles, and one title in mixed doubles. All of the success came in just four years. In July 1954, shortly after winning her third straight

Maureen Connolly took the tennis world by storm as a teenage phenom in the early 1950s.

Wimbledon title, Connolly was on a horseback ride when a cement truck struck her. Her right leg was broken, and she suffered severe damage to the muscles and nerves. She never played competitive tennis again.

SUNSHINE NETWORK
Cooper

UNLUCKY LINDROS

Hockey was defined by the grace and skill of Wayne Gretzky in the 1980s. Then Eric Lindros arrived on the scene with a game built on strength and speed. Lindros was the first pick in the 1991 National Hockey League (NHL) draft by the Quebec Nordiques. After a yearlong holdout he was traded to the Philadelphia Flyers, and in the fall of 1992 he hit the ice like a man on a mission.

The 6-foot-4, 240-pound center scored 41 goals in 61 games as a rookie. He added 44 goals and 53 assists in his second season. In just his third season Lindros won the Hart Trophy as the NHL MVP. He was on track to becoming the next big star at the center position. Two more 40-goal seasons followed, and he posted a career-high 115 points in 1995–96.

A hit by New Jersey defenseman Scott Stevens in the 2000 playoffs seriously affected Lindros's career. Lindros was carrying

Eric Lindros was a hard-charging forward for the Philadelphia Flyers.

Lindros's physical style of play led to numerous injuries in his career.

the puck down the ice when Stevens's shoulder hit Lindros in the head. Concussions had already taken their toll on Lindros. The hit by Stevens caused another concussion, and Lindros had a hard time recovering from its effects. Lindros played five more seasons for three different teams but was never the same. He was out of hockey after 13 seasons and 290 goals. Still, Lindros was inducted into the Hockey Hall of Fame in 2016.

DEATH ON THE ICE

Bill Masterton played 38 games for the Minnesota North Stars in 1967–68 in his only NHL season. He is the only player to die from injuries sustained in an NHL game. Masterton collided with another player and hit his head on the ice. Like most players from that era, he wasn't wearing a helmet. Masterton never regained consciousness. He died of a brain injury two days later at the age of 29.

Bill Masterton (19) played in just 38 games in his only season with the NHL's Minnesota North Stars.

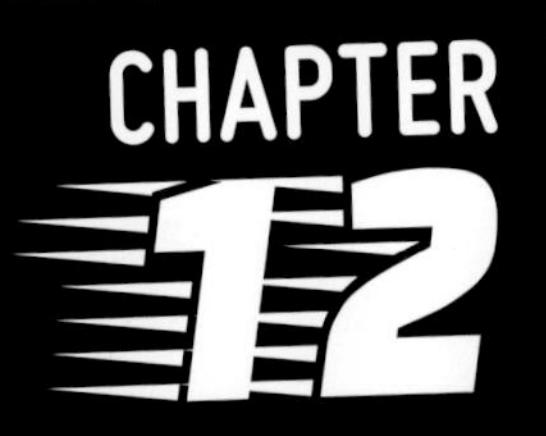

A HELPING HAND

Roberto Clemente was a dazzling outfielder with the Pittsburgh Pirates throughout an 18-year baseball career. He won one NL MVP Award, led the NL in hitting four times, and was awarded the Gold Glove for fielding excellence in each of the final 12 seasons of his career. But Clemente's story isn't complete without a discussion of his off-the-field contributions.

Away from the ballpark he was even more heroic. Clemente made his way to the major leagues from Puerto Rico, but he was beloved by all Latin Americans. In 1972 a powerful earthquake struck Nicaragua, and Clemente wanted to help. He was flying with supplies bound for the Central American country on December 31, 1972, when the heavily loaded plane crashed. He and four others died.

Clemente had doubled in his final at-bat of the 1972 season. That hit made him the 11th player in MLB history to reach the coveted

Roberto Clemente was a star outfielder for the Pittsburgh Pirates for 18 seasons.

3,000-hit mark. Upon his death, the Baseball Hall of Fame decided to waive the mandatory five-year waiting period, and Clemente was enshrined in 1973.

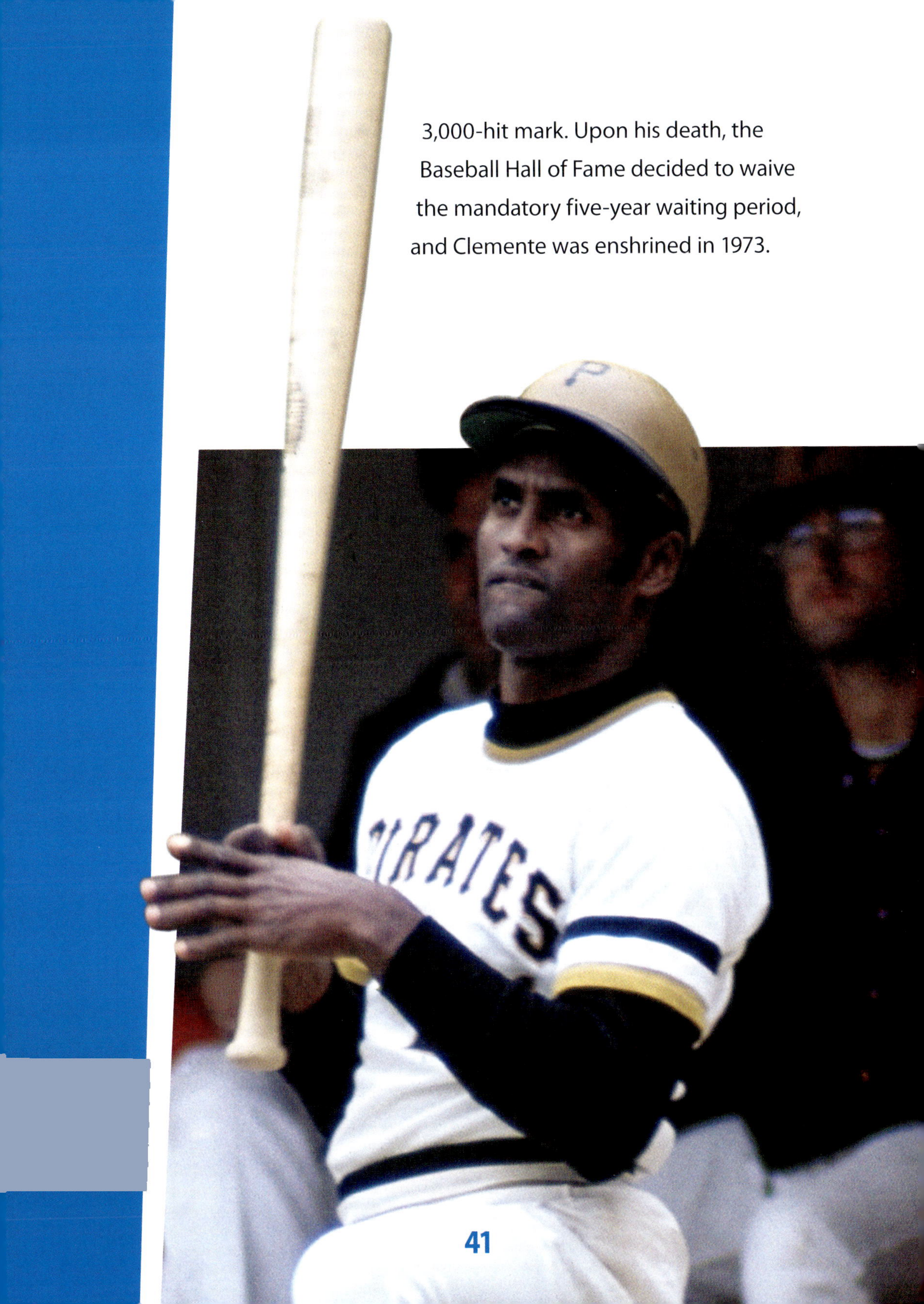

STANDING TALL

Most NBA teams use just one center on the floor at a time. The Houston Rockets decided to try something different. They made Ralph Sampson the first pick of the 1983 draft. Sampson stood 7 feet 4 inches tall and was a three-time Naismith Award winner at the University of Virginia. The next year, the Rockets added 7-foot center Hakeem Olajuwon and pioneered the "Twin Towers" approach.

Olajuwon would become one of the best NBA centers in history. Sampson became known for not living up to the hype. Sampson averaged 16.9 points and 11.4 rebounds per game in his four outstanding seasons at Virginia.

At first it appeared Sampson would make a smooth transition to the NBA. He averaged 21.0 points, 11.1 rebounds, 2.4 blocks, and 2.0 assists per game in 1983–84 and was named NBA Rookie of the Year. He posted similar stats the next two seasons, but then a back injury

Ralph Sampson (50) goes up to defend a shot against 7-foot-4-inch Mark Eaton of the Utah Jazz.

triggered a downslide of his career. The bad back led to knee injuries, and Sampson's career ended after he had played just 456 games in nine seasons.

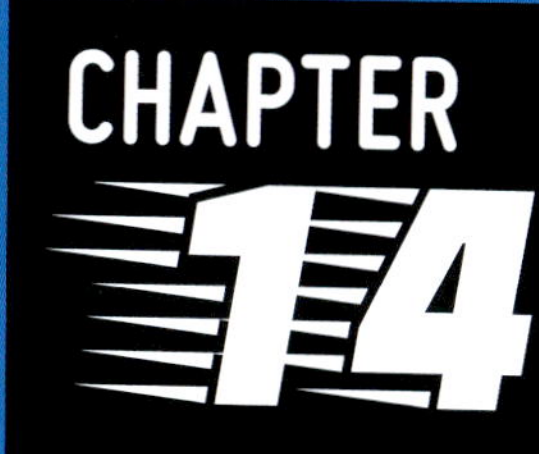

SHOELESS JOE

Outfielder "Shoeless" Joe Jackson played 13 years in the major leagues. He never won an MVP award and wasn't inducted into the Hall of Fame. But his name will always be remembered. He was part of the "Black Sox" scandal of 1919. He and seven of his Chicago White Sox teammates were banned from baseball after being accused of taking money to lose the World Series on purpose.

Jackson was one of the best hitters of his time. He hit .408 in 1911, twice led the AL in hits, and led the league in triples three times. Jackson and the White Sox won the World Series in 1917.

Two years later Chicago was the favorite to win it again. But the Cincinnati Reds pulled off an upset. Later, eight of the White Sox players were accused of taking money from gamblers. Jackson admitted he took the money but said he didn't try to lose. He hit .375 and had the only home run of the series. That didn't matter to baseball's new commissioner, Kenesaw Mountain Landis. Jackson and the other seven players were banned from baseball for life.

Shoeless Joe Jackson had a lifetime batting average of .356, but he was banned from baseball in the wake of the infamous Black Sox scandal.

GLOSSARY

commissioner

The chief executive of a sports league.

contract

An agreement to play for a certain team.

draft

A system that allows teams to acquire new players coming into a league.

dynasty

A team that has an extended period of success, usually winning multiple championships in the process.

elusive

Difficult to catch or contain.

enlist

To voluntarily join an organization, typically the military.

friendly fire

An attack by the military on one of its own members while attempting to engage with the enemy.

mandatory

Required.

pioneer

To become the first to attempt something new or unusual.

prospect

A young player expected to become a star.

scandal

An action or event regarded as morally or legally wrong and causing general public outrage.

upset

An unexpected victory by a supposedly weaker player or team.

ONLINE RESOURCES

To learn more about athletes whose careers were cut short, visit **abdobooklinks.com**. These links are routinely monitored and updated to provide the most current information available.

MORE INFORMATION

BOOKS

Buckley, James, Jr. *Lou Gehrig: Iron Horse of Baseball.* New York: Sterling, 2010.

Campbell, Dave. *The Most Notorious Curses of All Time.* Minneapolis, MN: Abdo Publishing, 2016.

Gitlin, Marty. *Sports' Most Memorable Characters.* Minneapolis, MN: Abdo Publishing, 2018.

INDEX

ABOUT THE AUTHOR

Brian Hall is a sports reporter who graduated from the University of Minnesota following a stint in the US Army. He lives in Minnesota with his wife and two kids.